ELEPHANT

PRACTICE AS SHOWN

ELEPHANT

PRACTICE AS SHOWN

ELEPHANT
PRACTICE AS SHOWN
PRACTICE AS SHOWN

ELEPHANT
DRAW THE MISSING LEVEL 1

ELEPHANT
DRAW THE MISSING LEVEL 2

CONNECT THE DOTS 1 TO 40

ELEPHANT

ELEPHANT

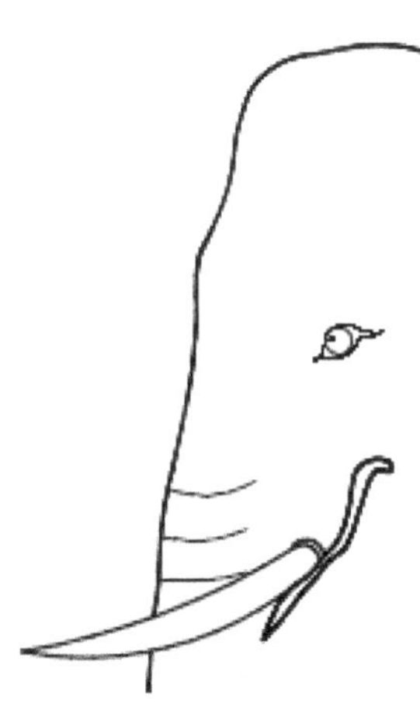

DRAW AS SHOWN ABOVE

CAT

PRACTICE AS SHOWN

CAT

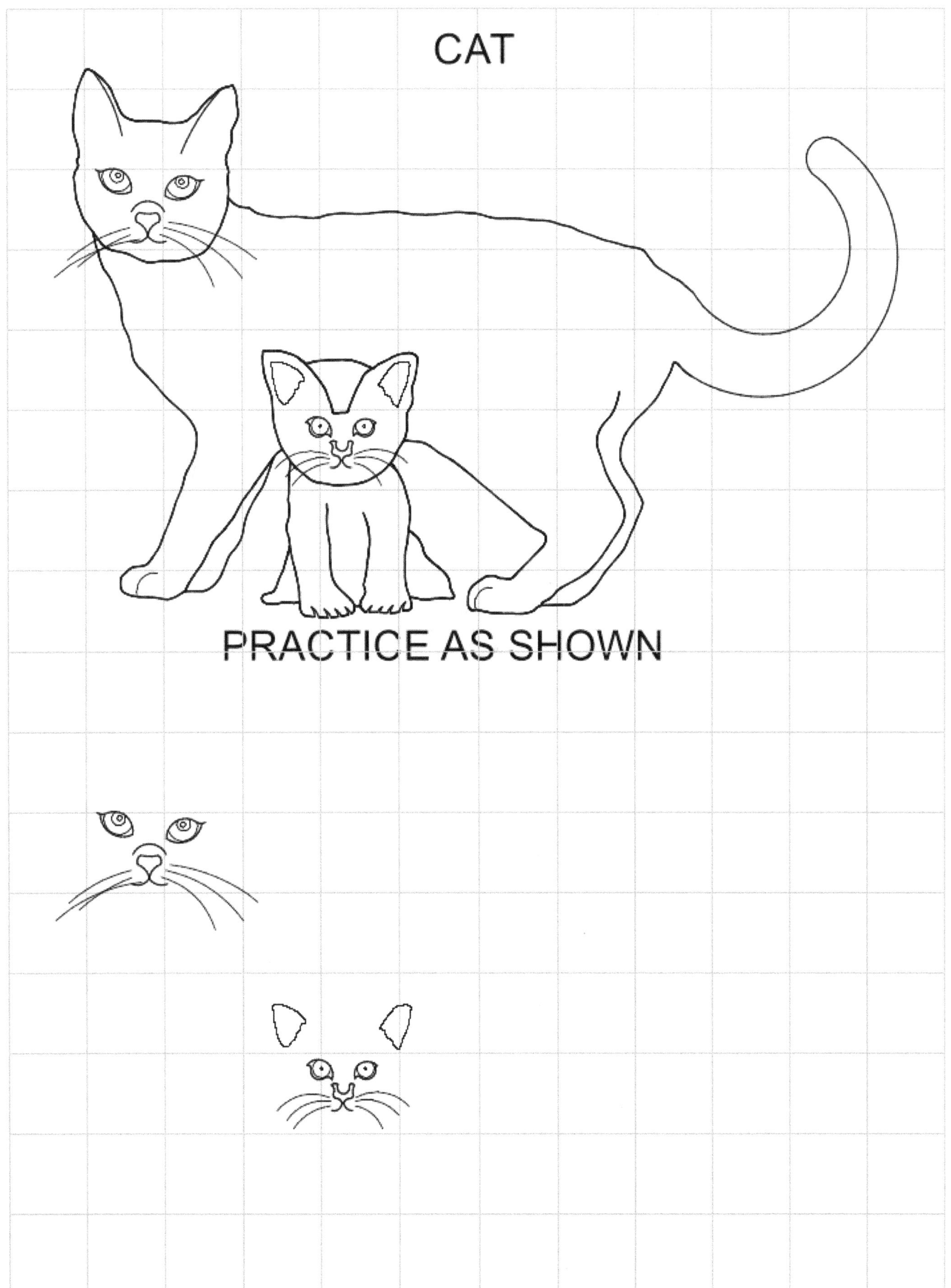

CAT

PRACTICE AS SHOWN

CAT

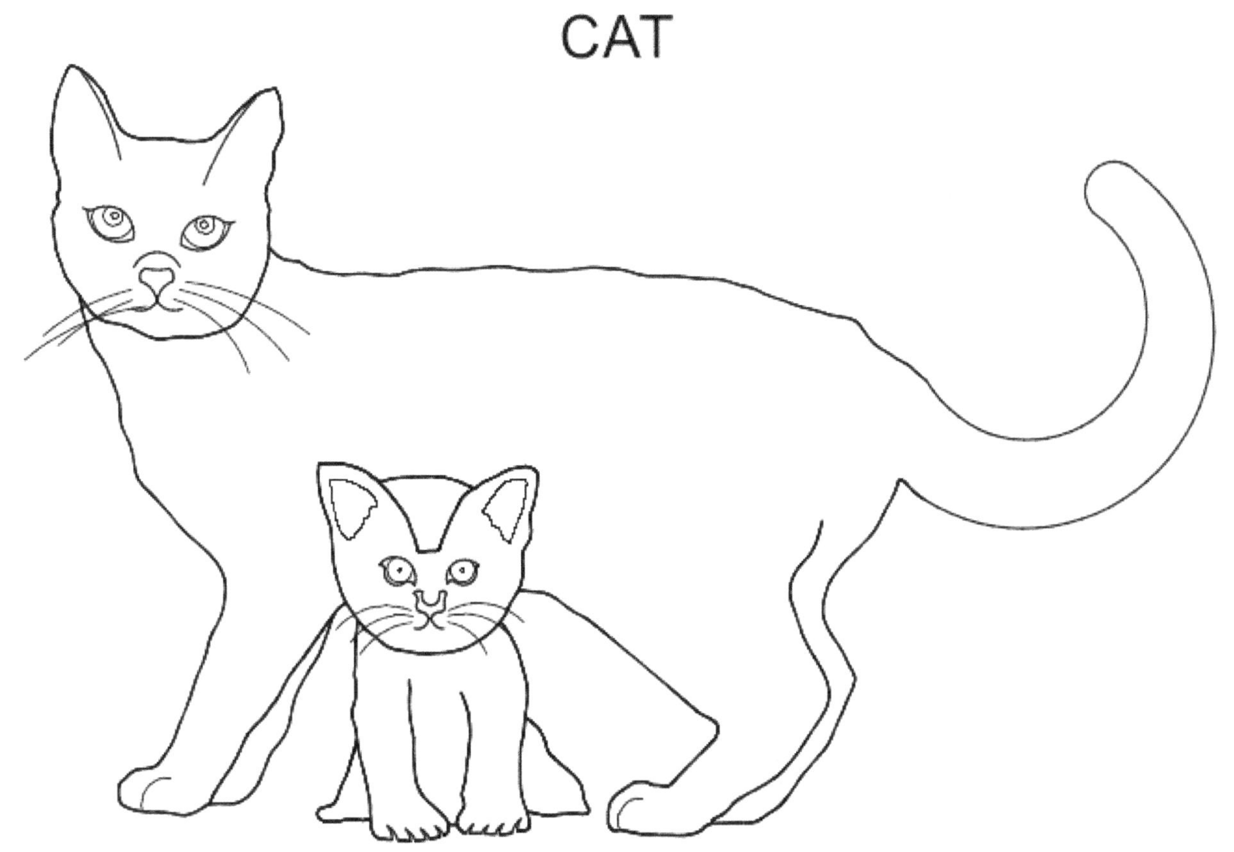

DRAW THE MISSING LEVEL 1

CAT

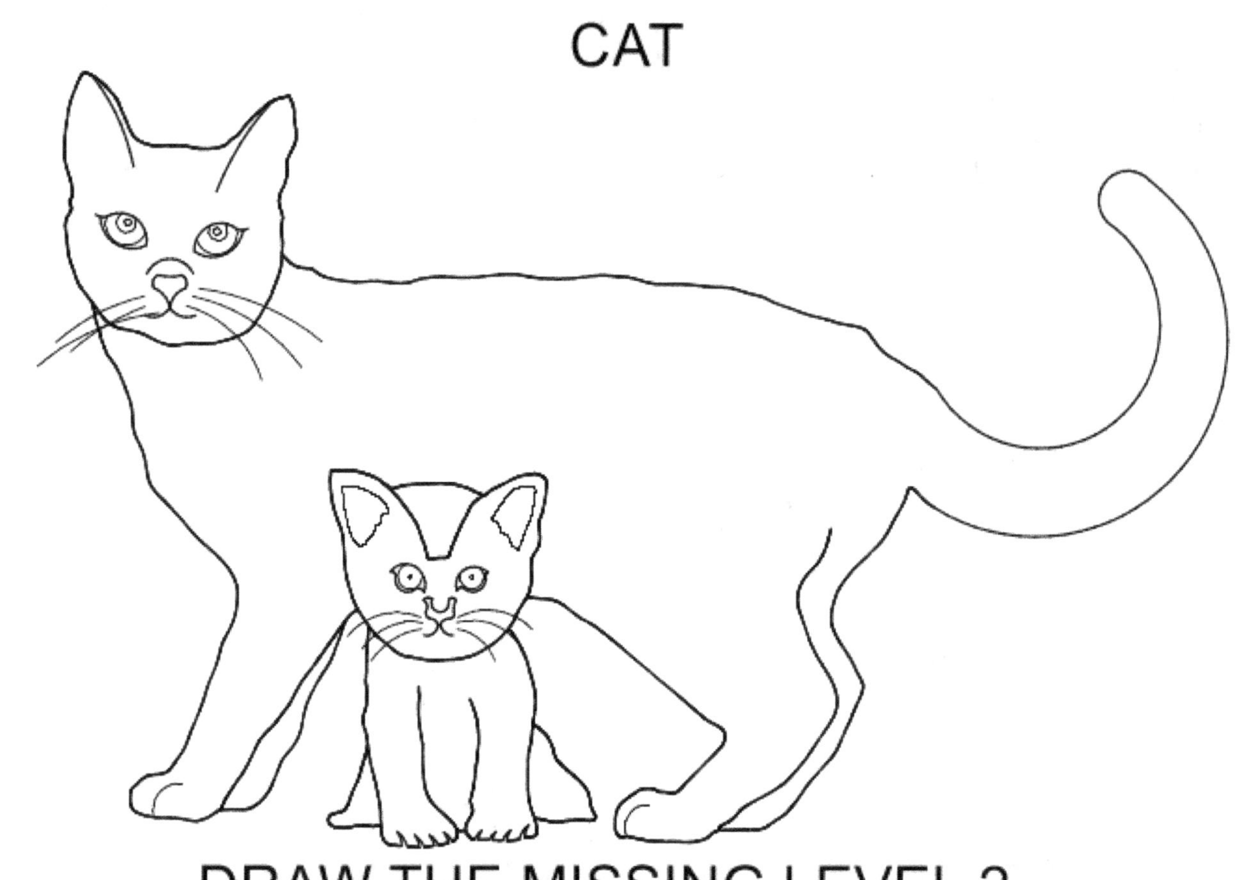

DRAW THE MISSING LEVEL 2

CONNECT THE DOTS 1 TO 51

CAT

CAT

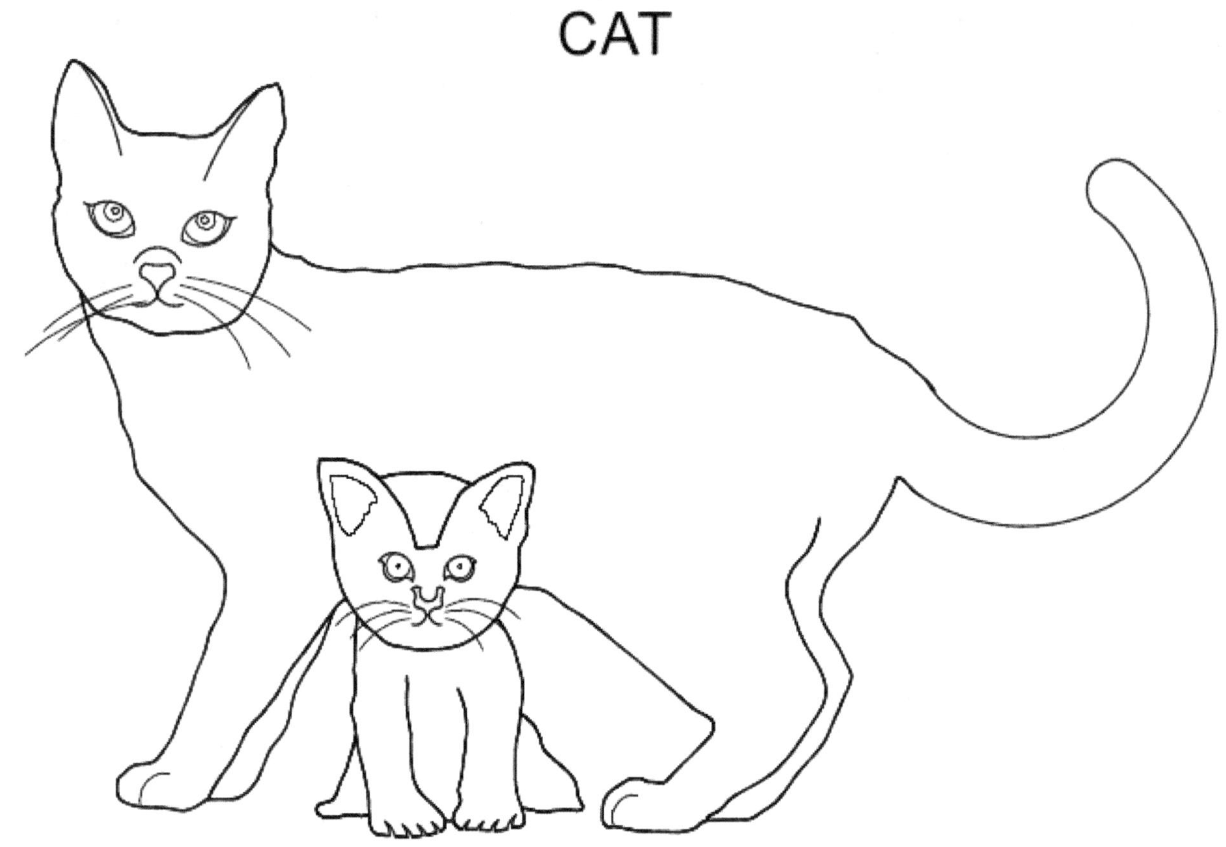

DRAW AS SHOWN ABOVE

CAMEL
PRACTICE AS SHOWN

CAMEL

CAMEL
PRACTICE AS SHOWN

DRAW THE MISSING LEVEL 1

DRAW THE MISSING LEVEL 2

CONNECT THE DOTS 1 TO 48

CAMEL

DRAW AS SHOWN ABOVE

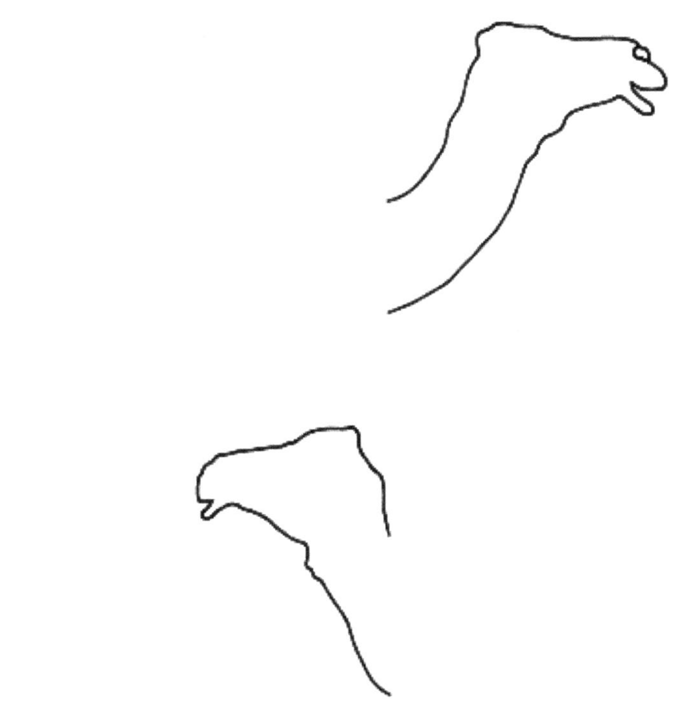

HORSE

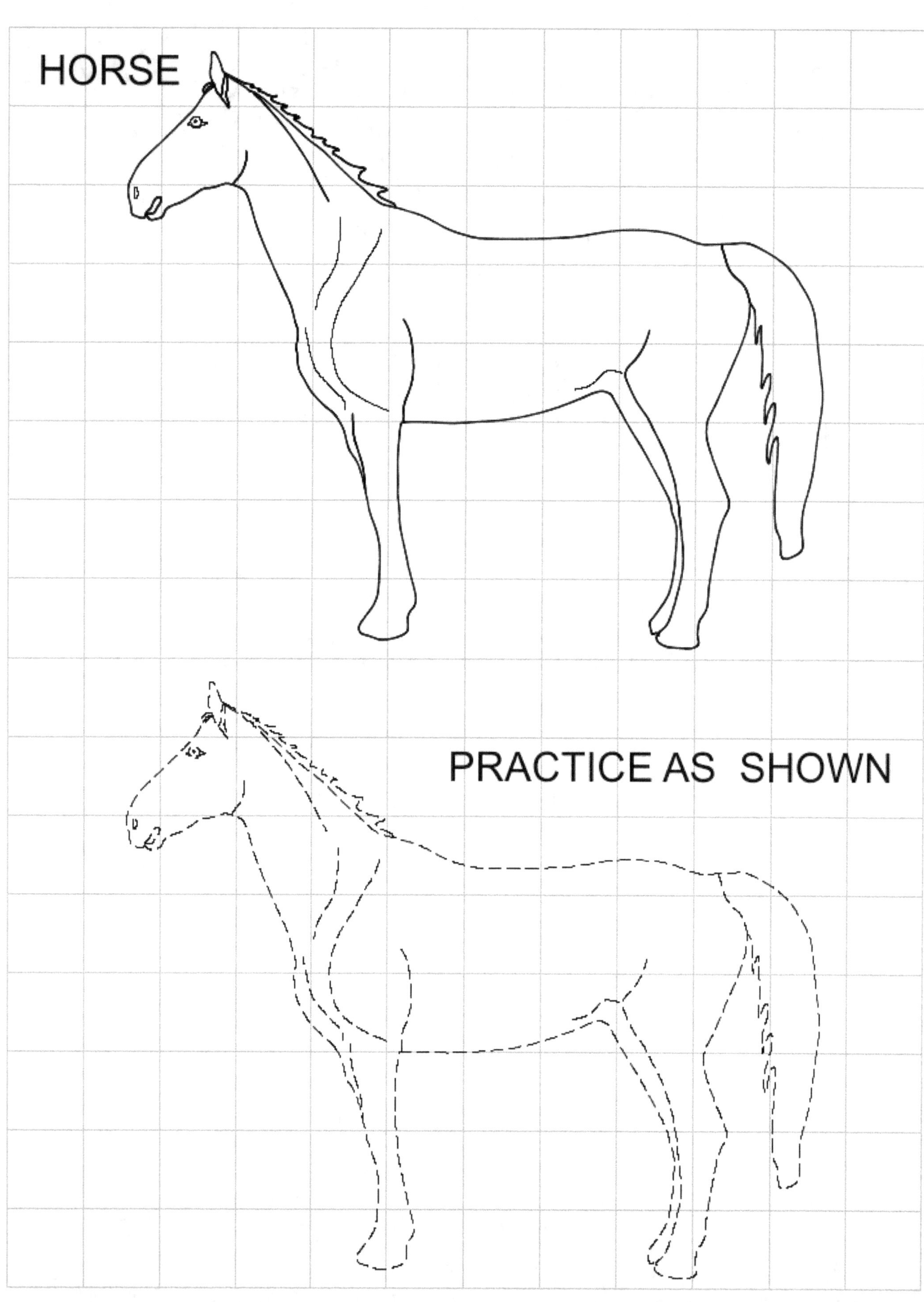

PRACTICE AS SHOWN

HORSE

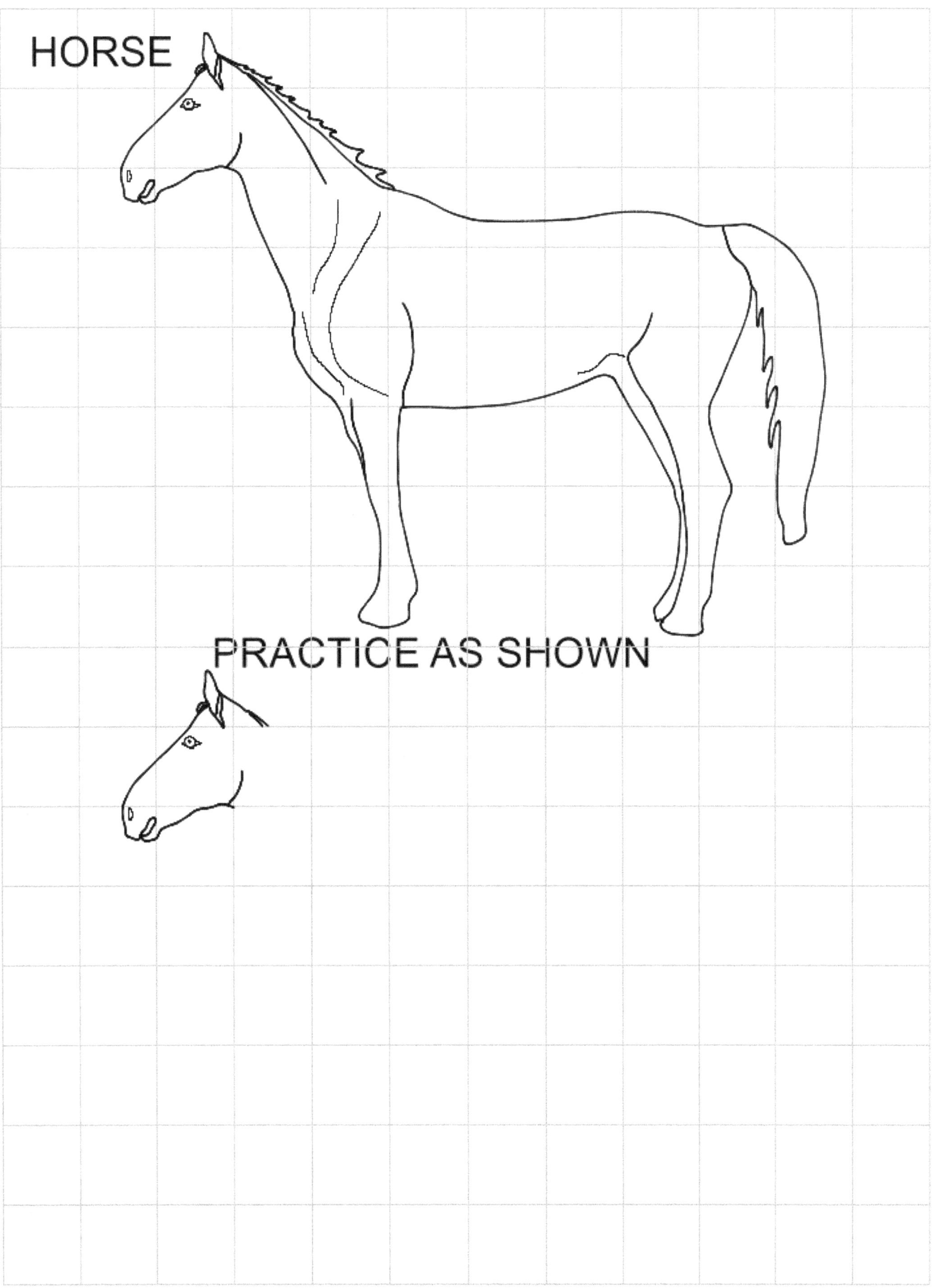

HORSE
PRACTICE AS SHOWN

HORSE

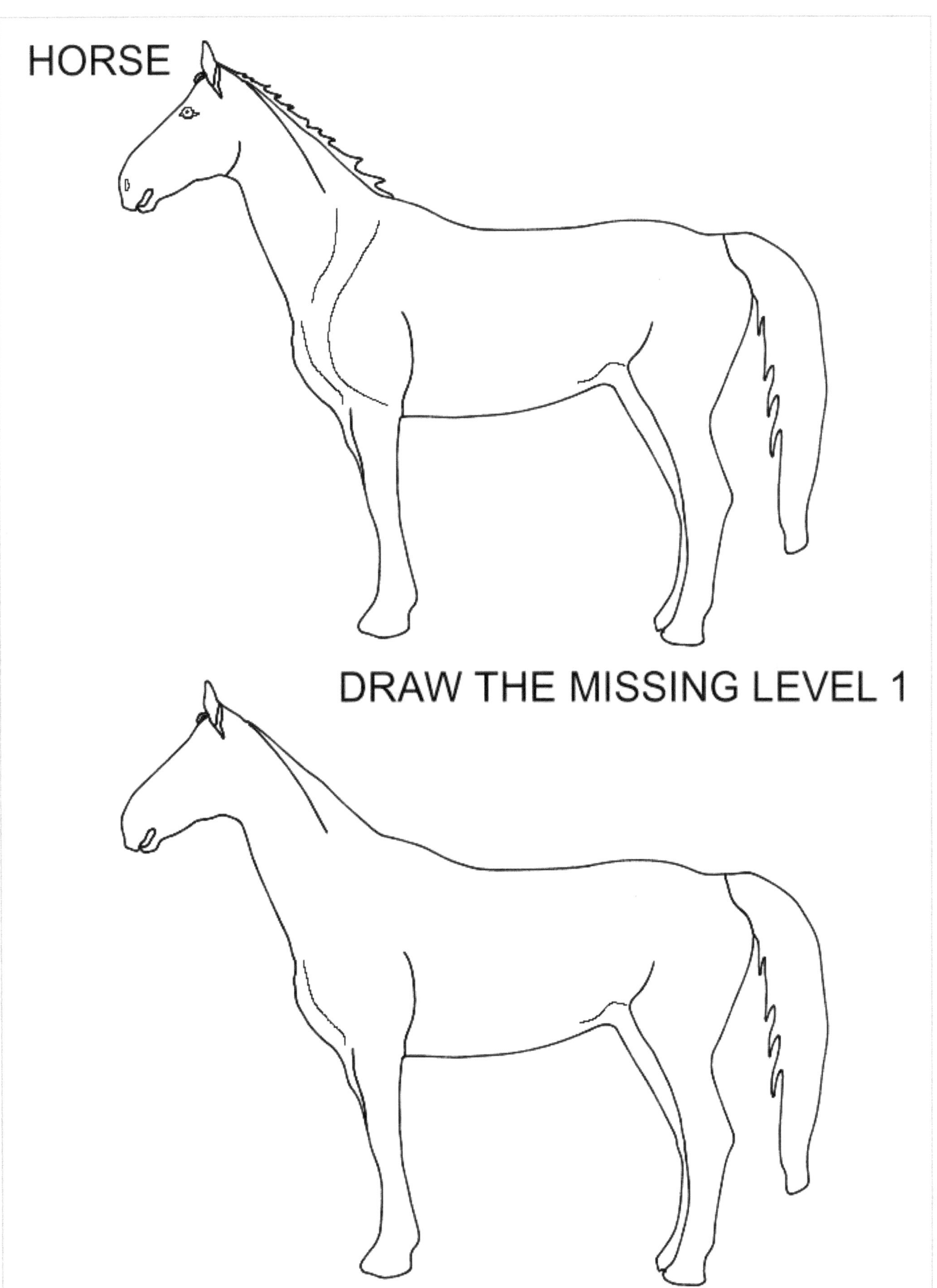

HORSE

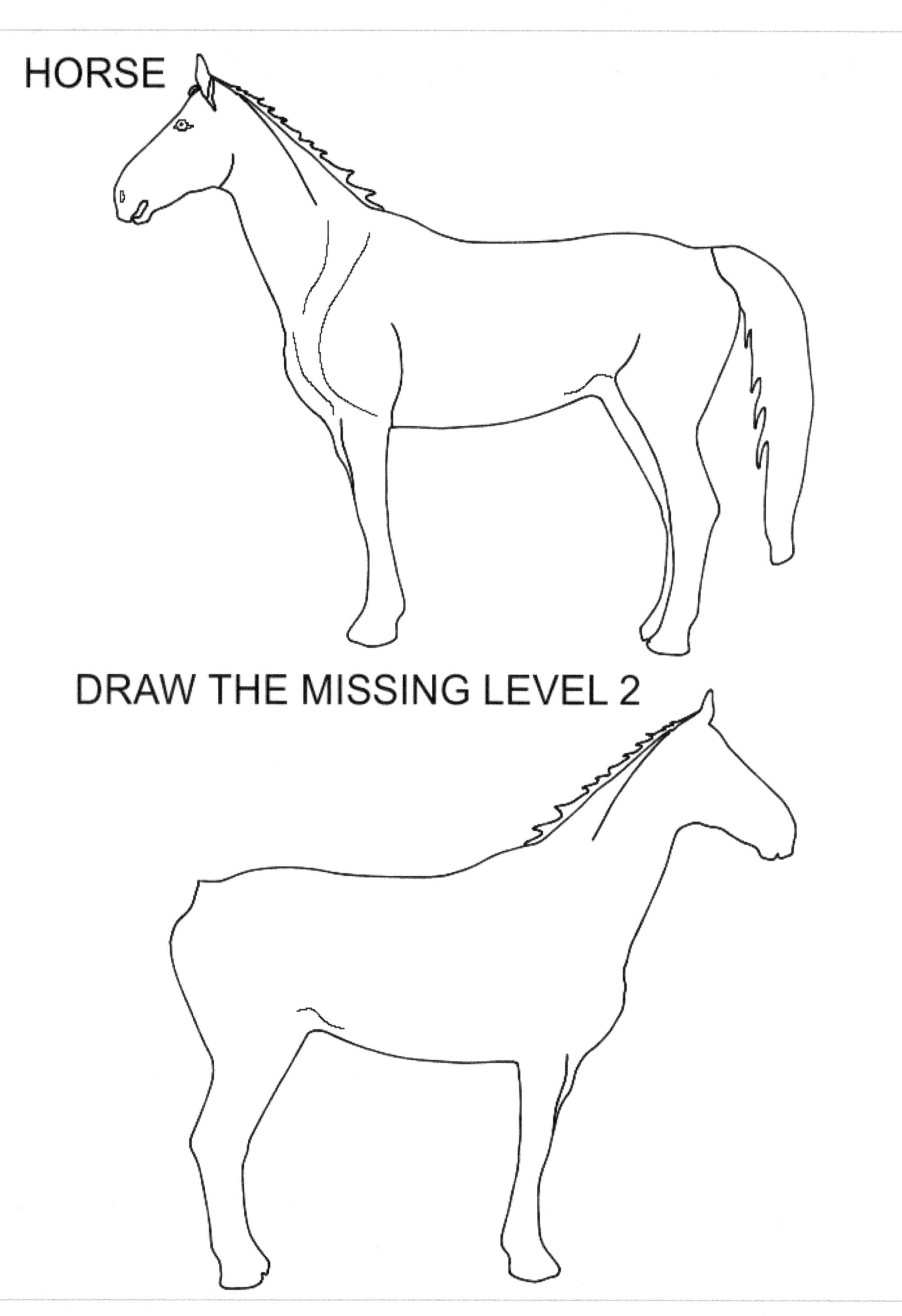

CONNECT THE DOTS 1 TO 50

HORSE

HORSE

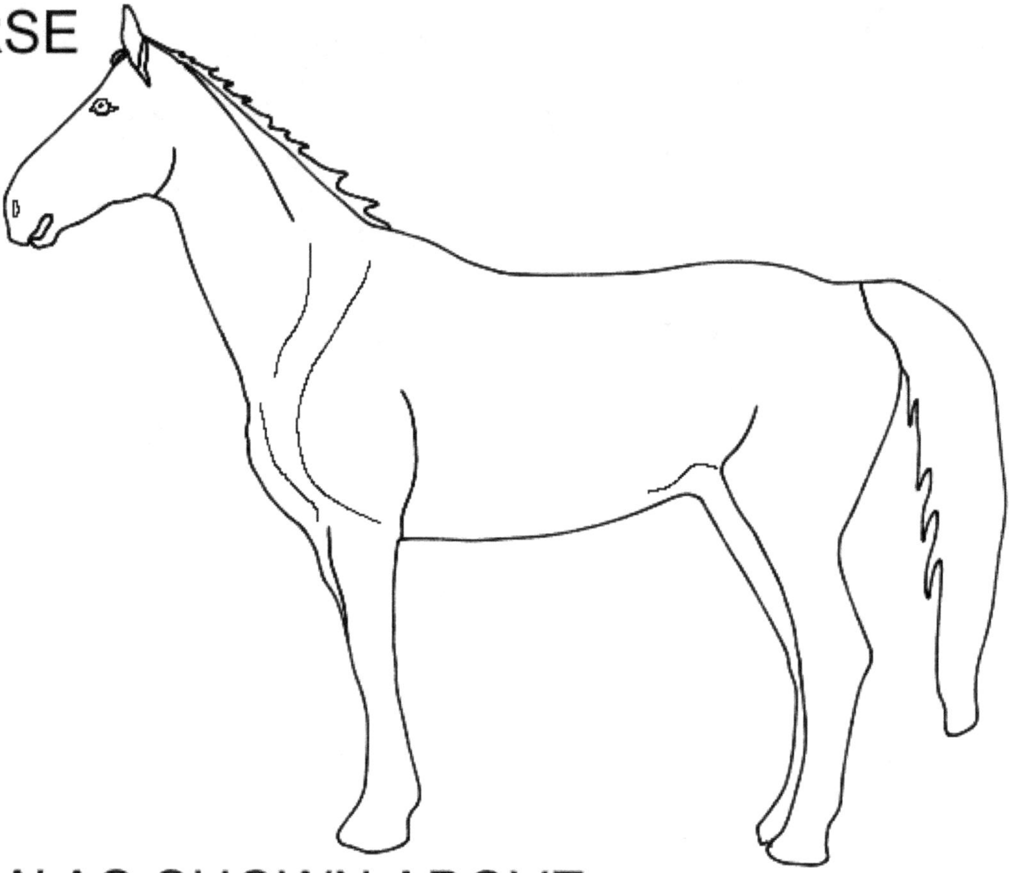

DRAW AS SHOWN ABOVE

GIANT PANDA

PRACTICE AS SHOWN

GIANT PANDA
PRACTICE AS SHOWN

GIANT PANDA

PRACTICE AS SHOWN

GIANT PANDA

DRAW THE MISSING LEVEL 1

GIANT PANDA

DRAW THE MISSING LEVEL 2

CONNECT THE DOTS 1 TO 27
GIANT PANDA

GIANT PANDA

DRAW AS SHOWN ABOVE

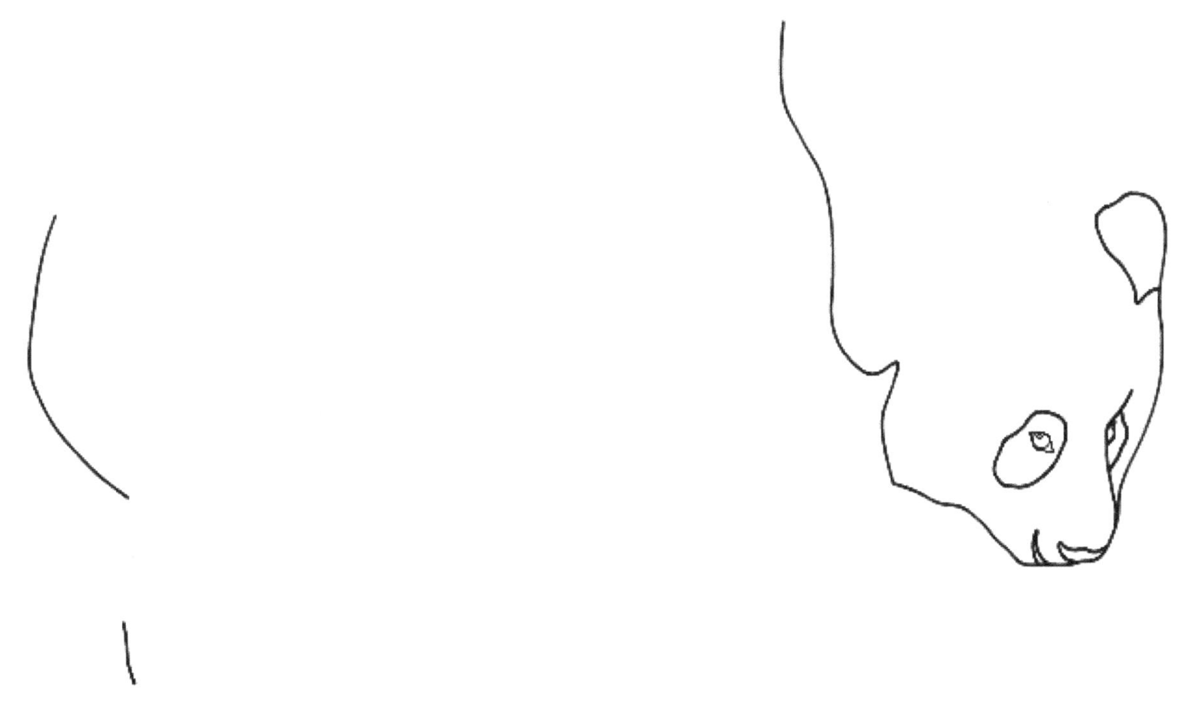

LION

PRACTICE
AS SHOWN

LION

PRACTICE
AS SHOWN

LION

PRACTICE
AS SHOWN

LION
DRAW THE
MISSING
LEVEL 1

LION
DRAW THE
MISSING
LEVEL 2

CONNECT THE
DOTS 1 TO 19

LION

LION

DRAW AS SHOWN
ABOVE

GIRAFFE

PRACTICE
AS SHOWN

GIRAFFE

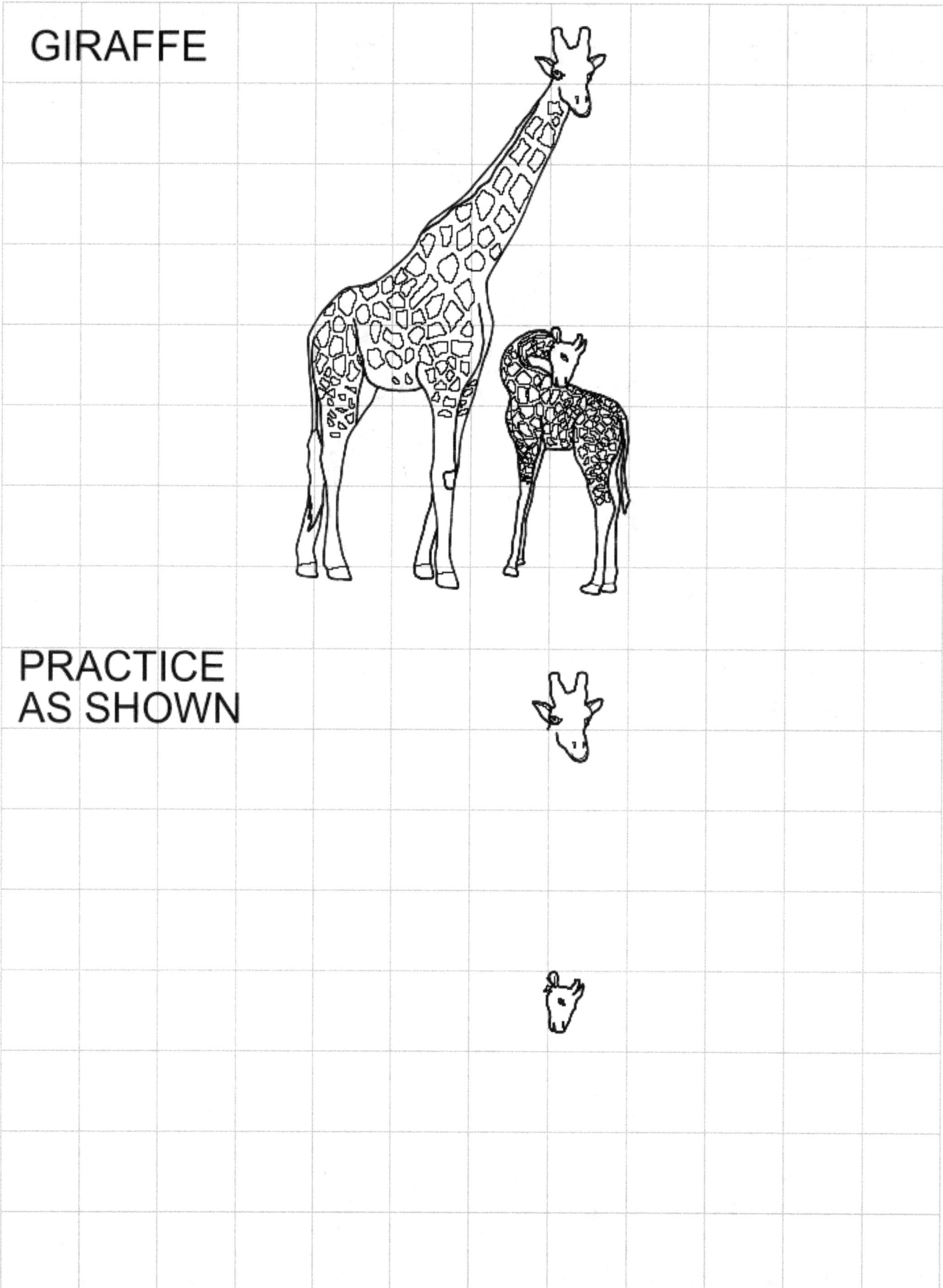

PRACTICE
AS SHOWN

GIRAFFE

PRACTICE
AS SHOWN

GIRAFFE

DRAW THE
MISSING
LEVEL 1

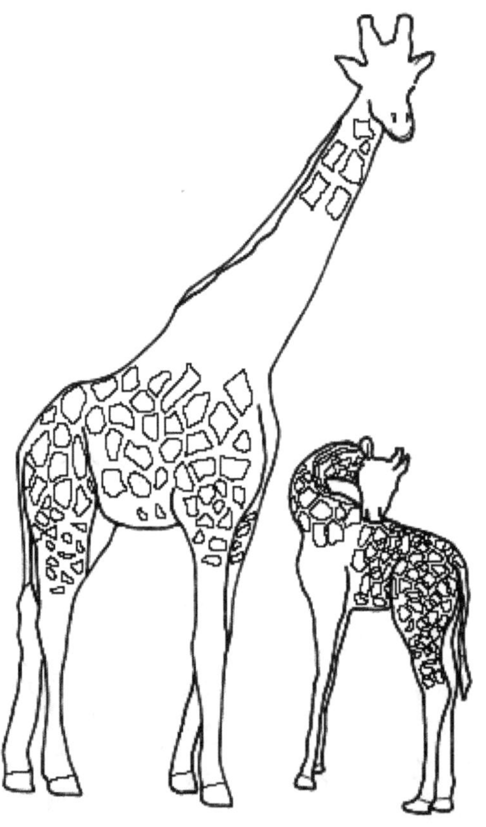

GIRAFFE

DRAW THE
MISSING
LEVEL 2

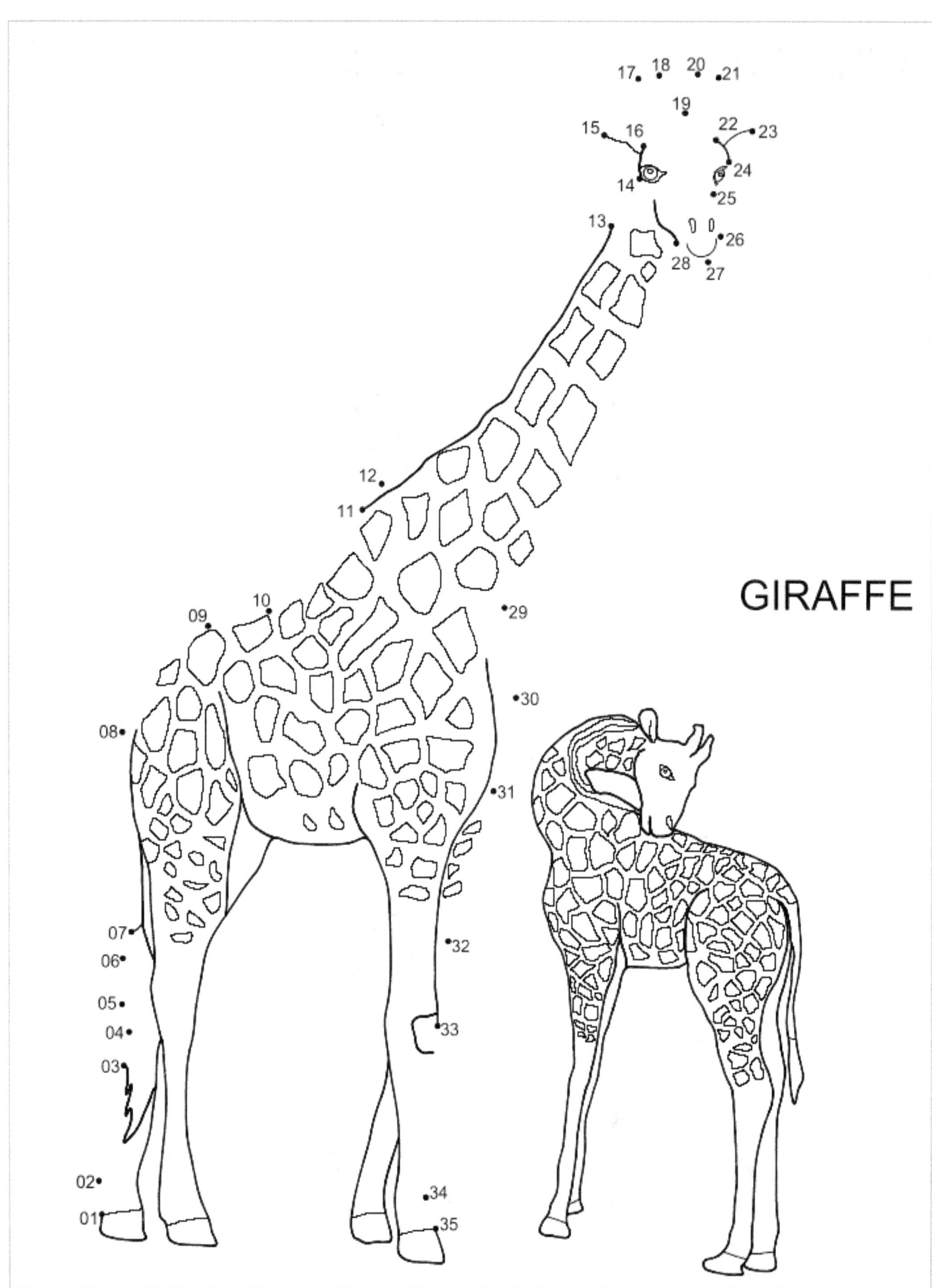
GIRAFFE

GIRAFFE

DRAW AS SHOWN
ABOVE

MONKEY

PRACTICE AS SHOWN

MONKEY

PRACTICE AS SHOWN

MONKEY
PRACTICE AS SHOWN

MONKEY

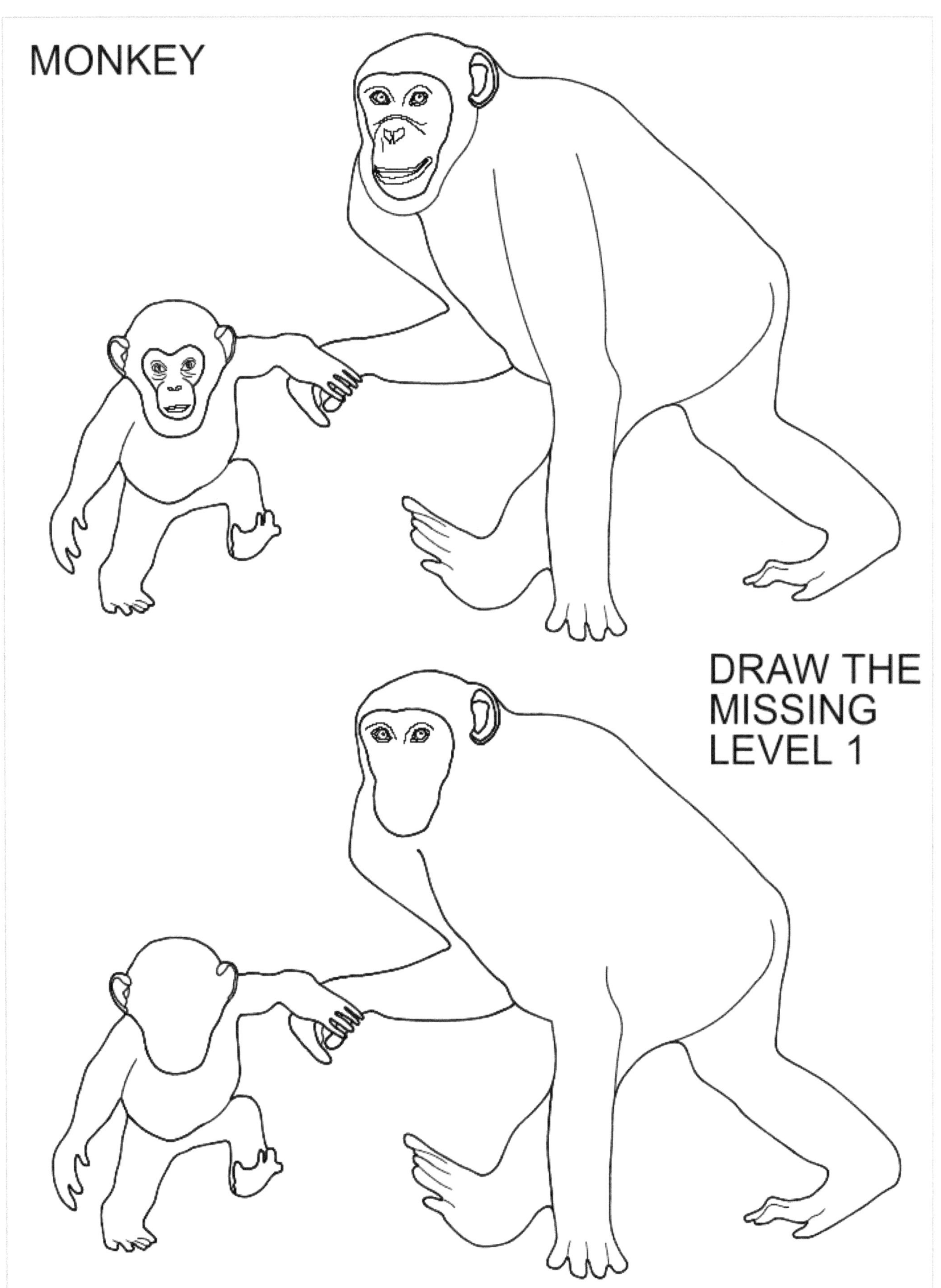

MONKEY

MONKEY
DRAW THE
MISSING
LEVEL 2

CONNECT THE DOTS 1 TO 32

MONKEY

MONKEY

DRAW AS SHOWN
ABOVE

TURTLE

PRACTICE AS SHOWN

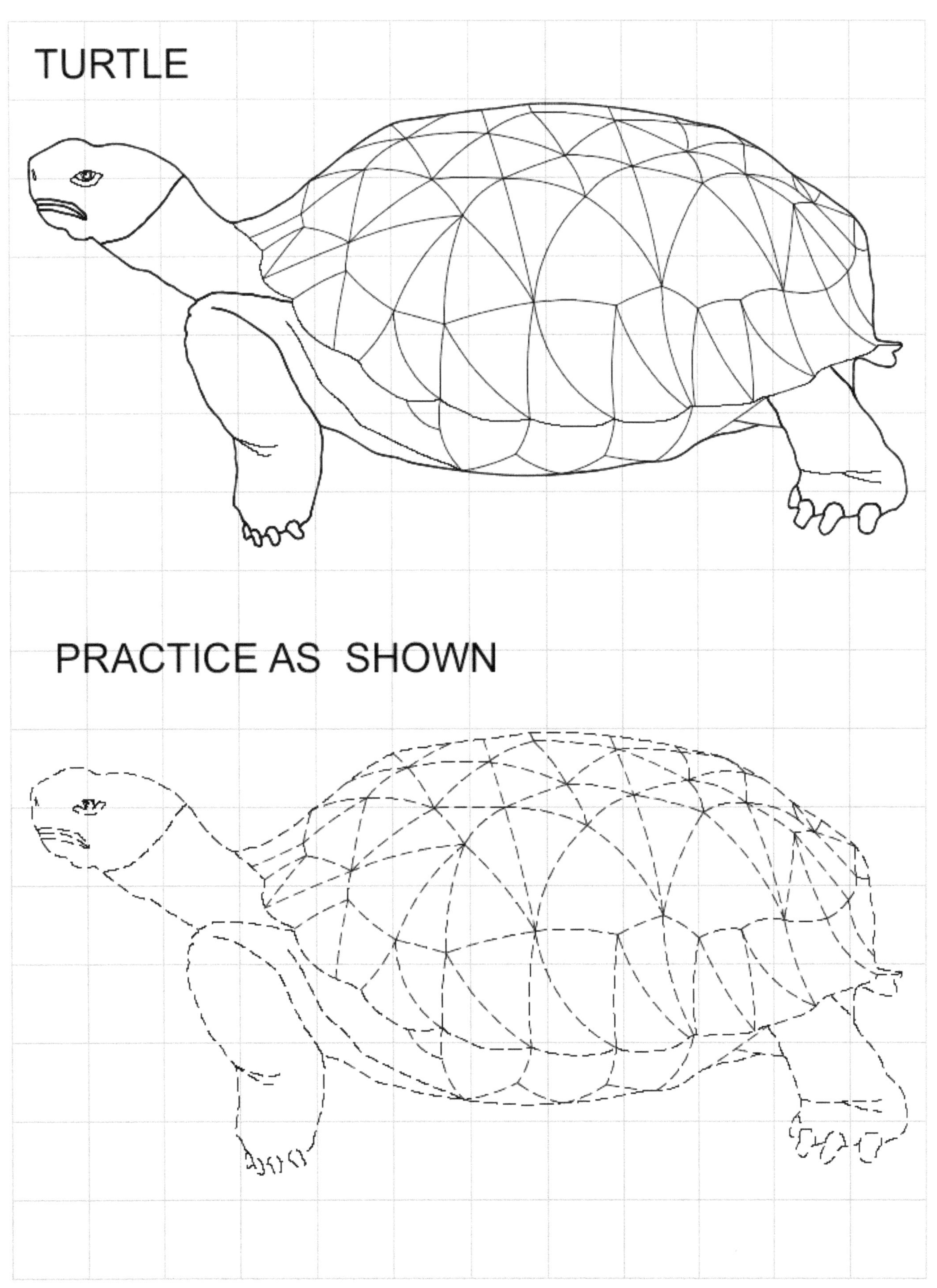

TURTLE

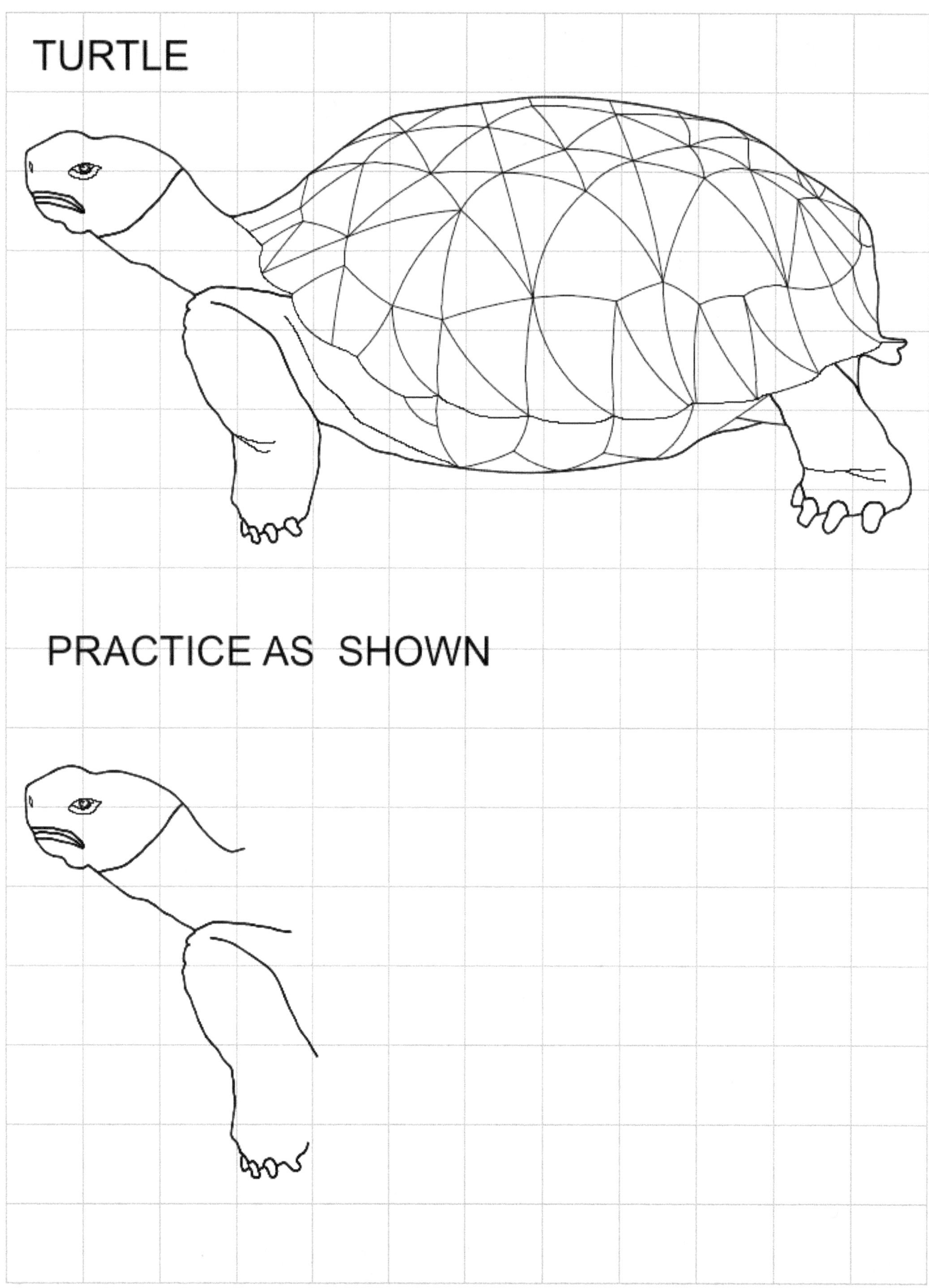

TURTLE

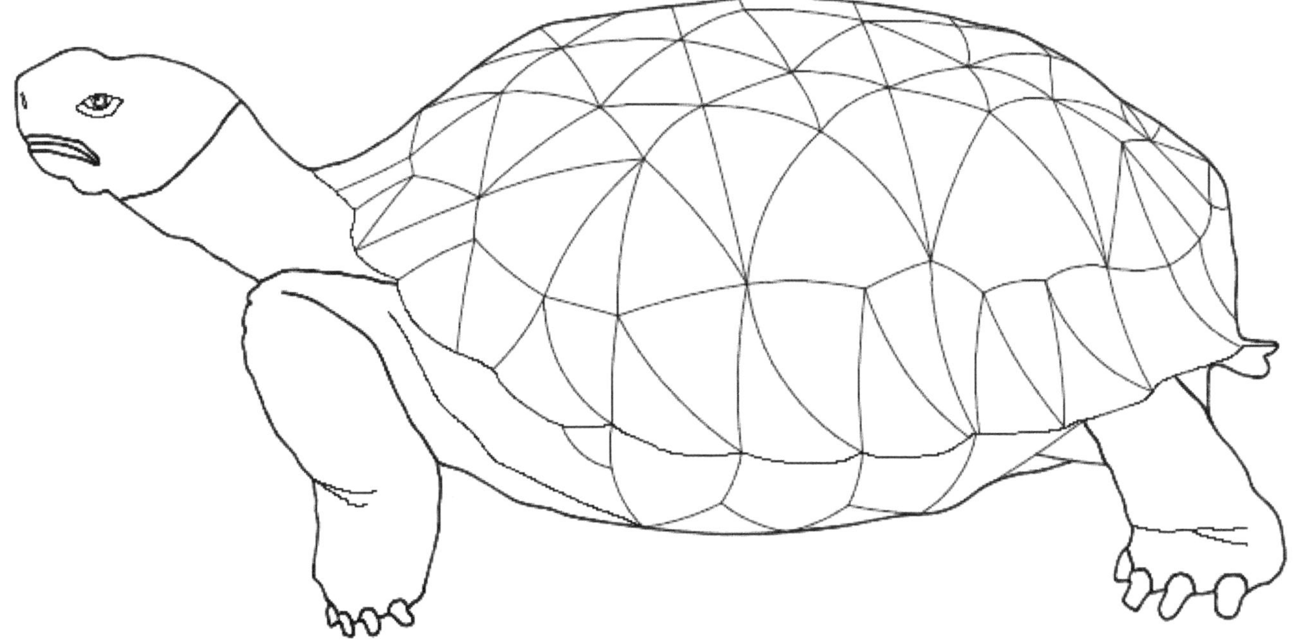

PRACTICE AS SHOWN

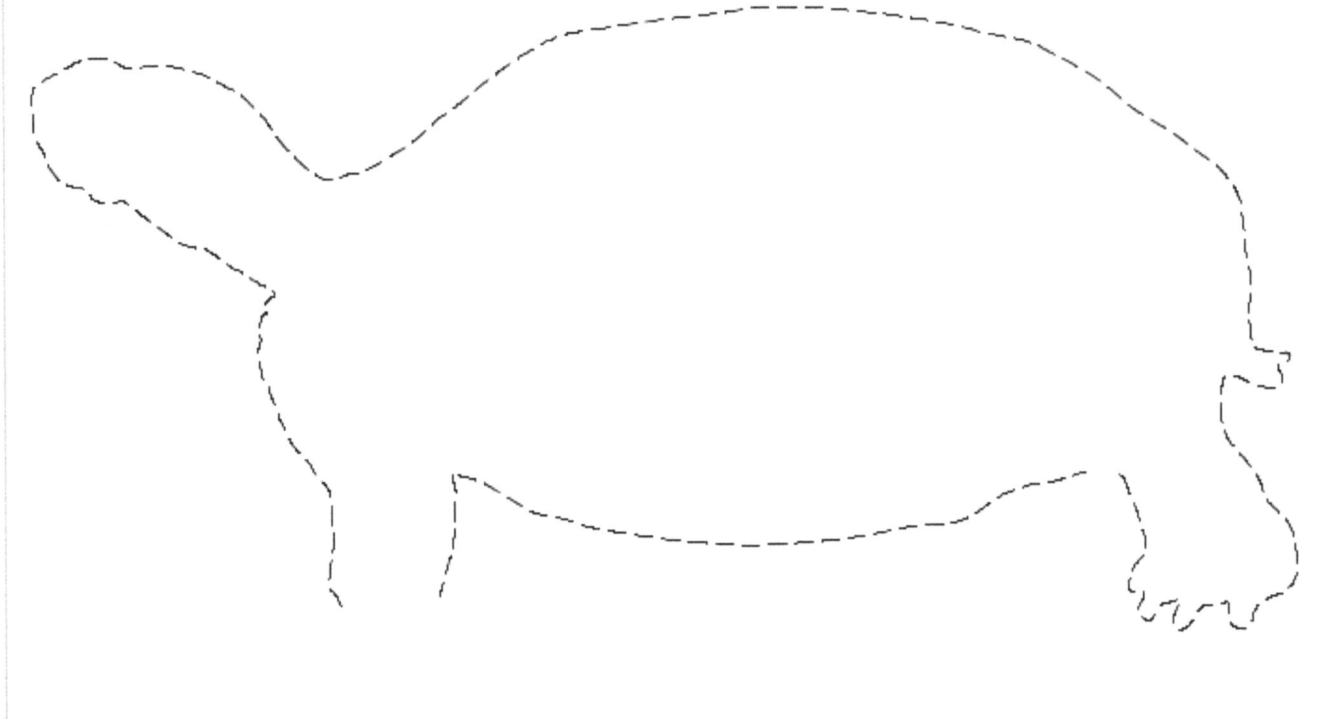

TURTLE

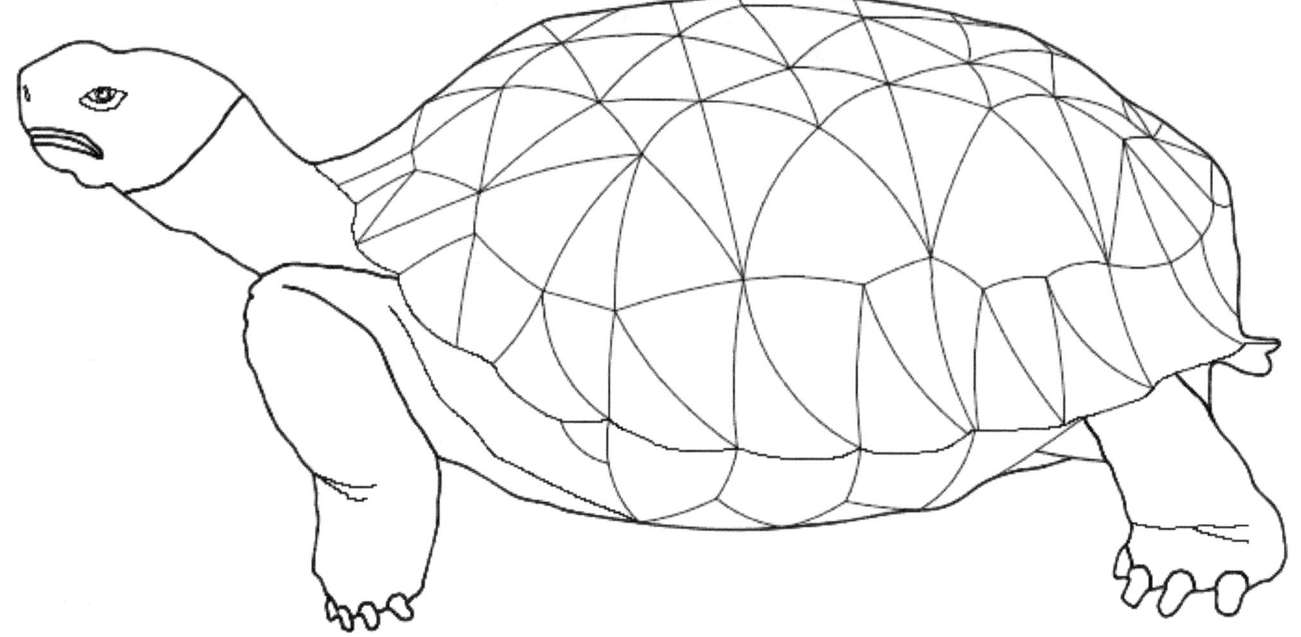

DRAW THE MISSING LEVEL 1

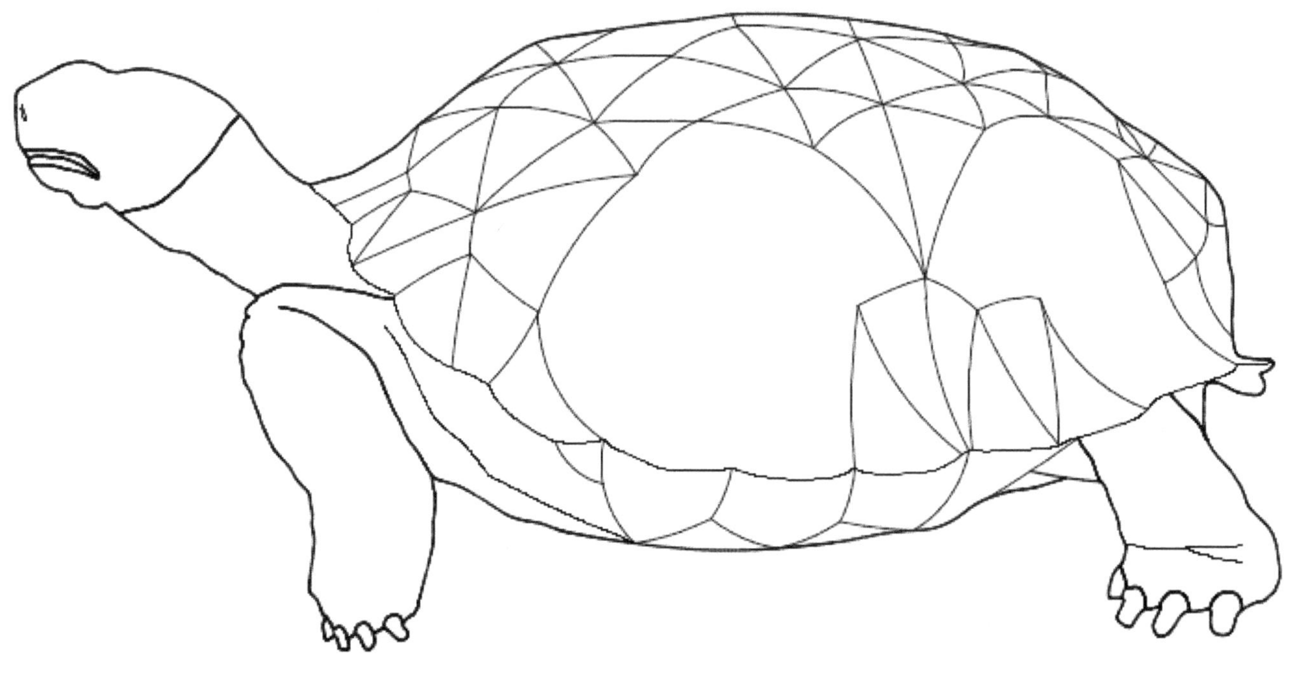

TURTLE

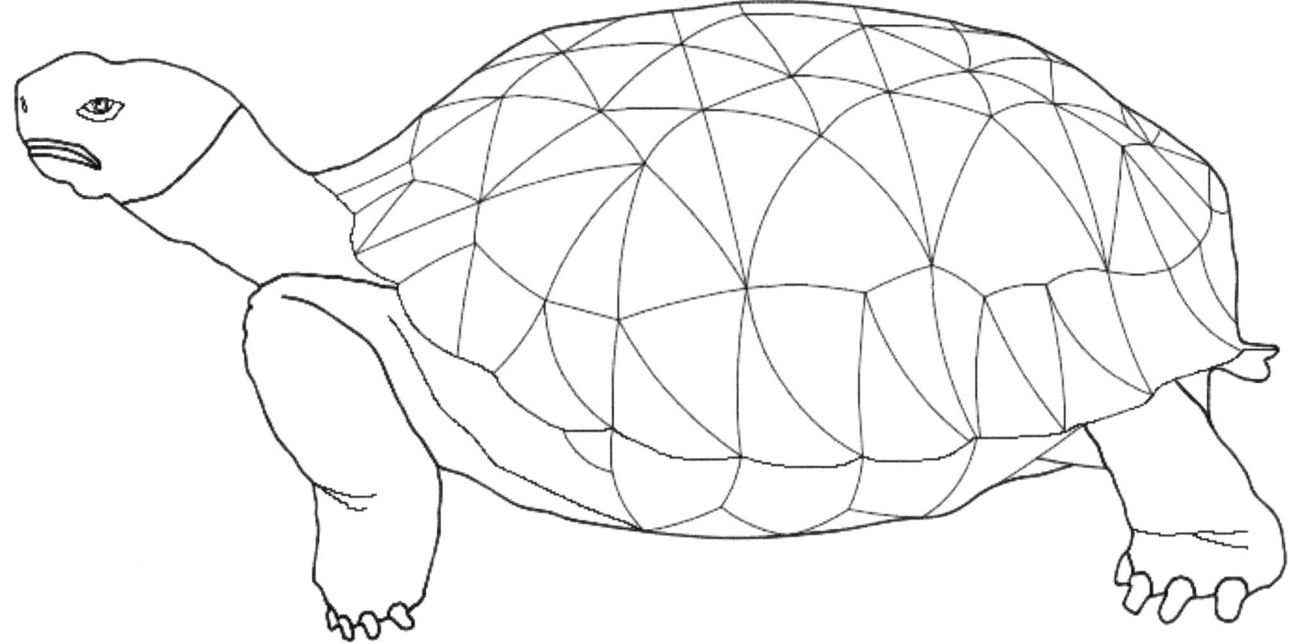

DRAW THE MISSING LEVEL 2

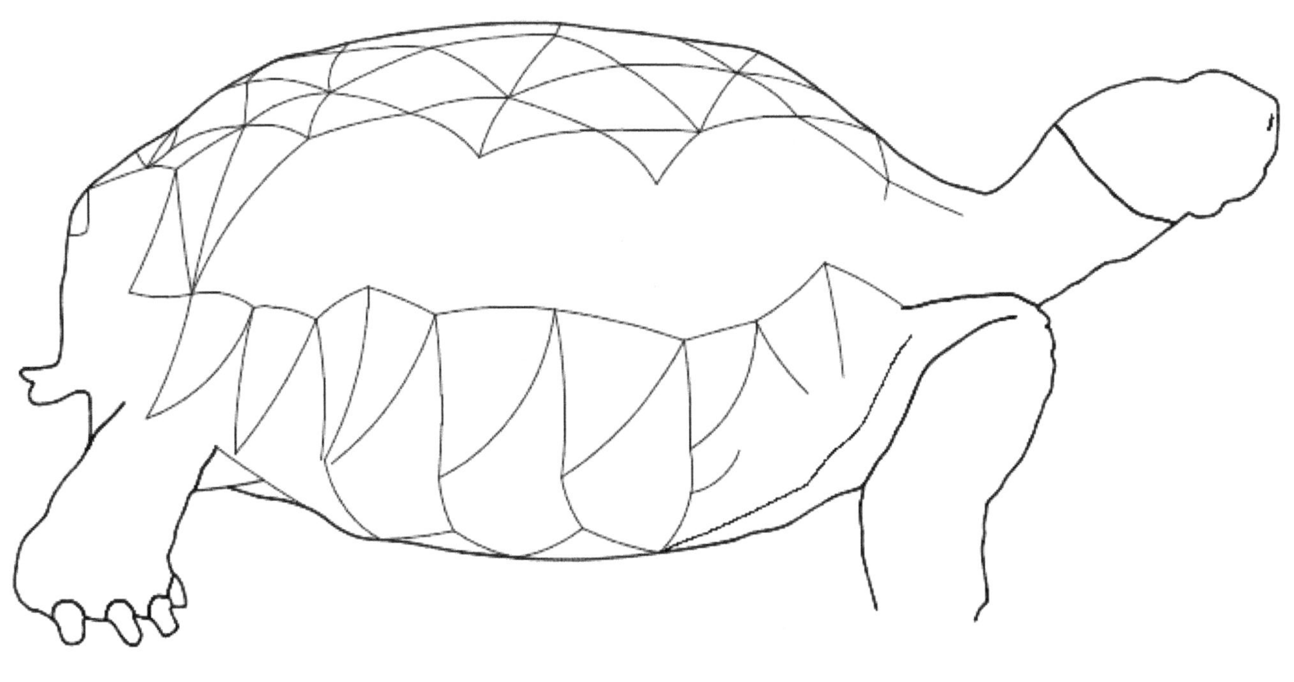

CONNECT THE DOTS 1 TO 32

TURTLE

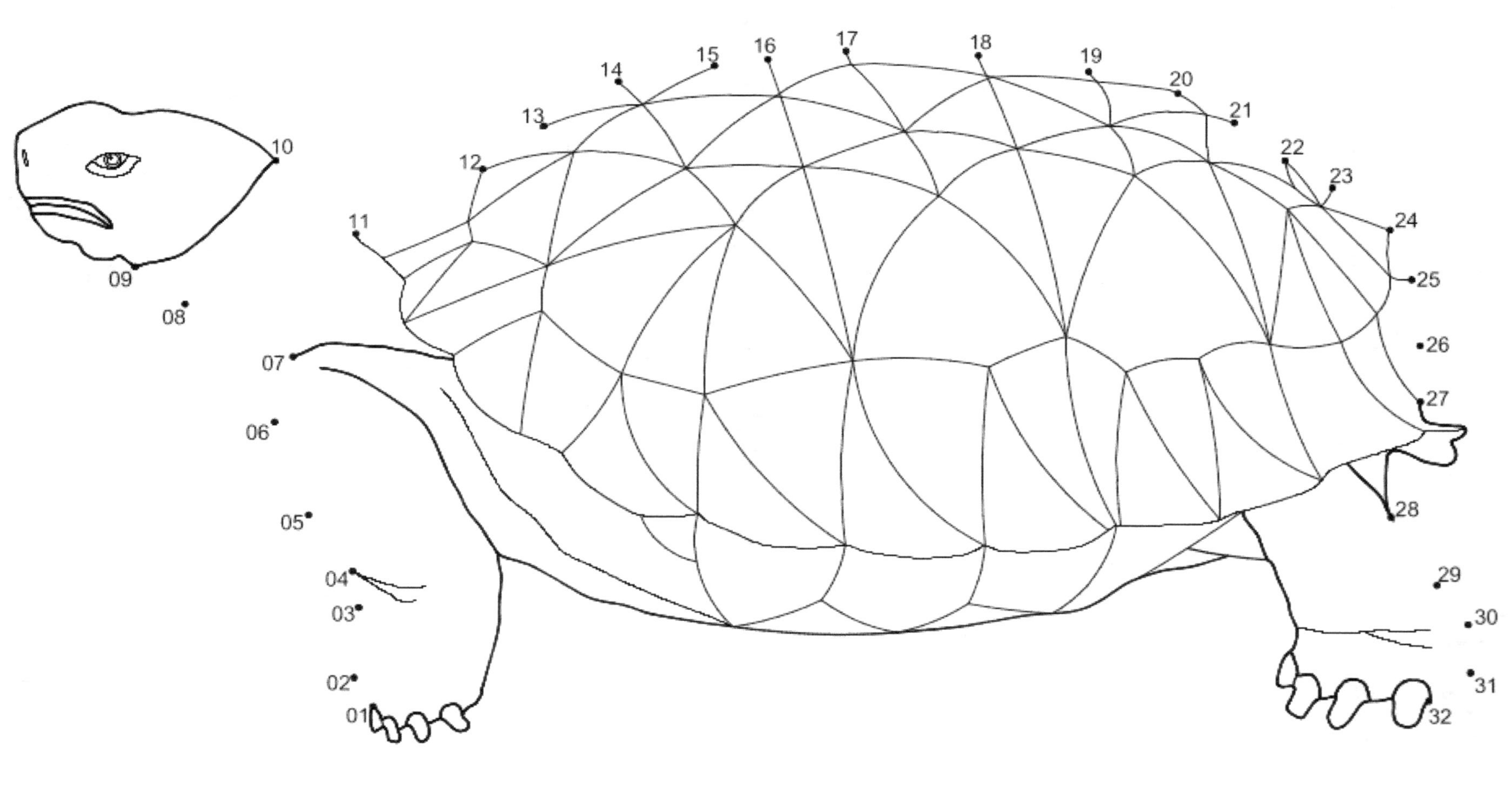

TURTLE

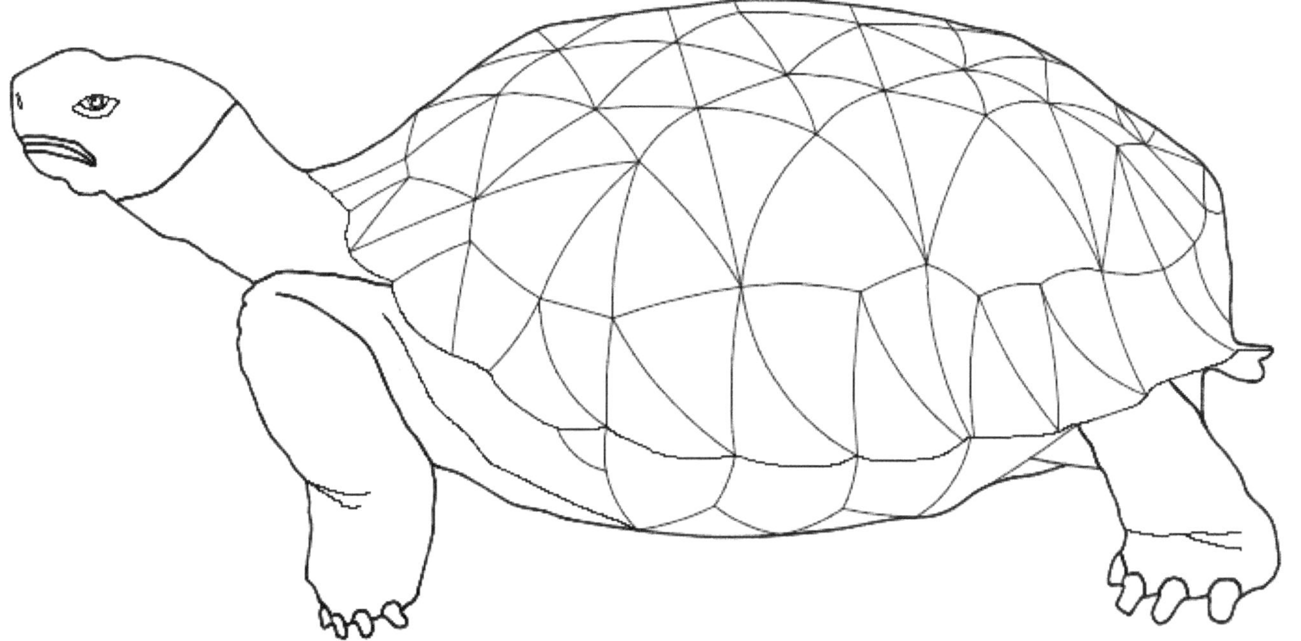

PRACTICE AS SHOWN

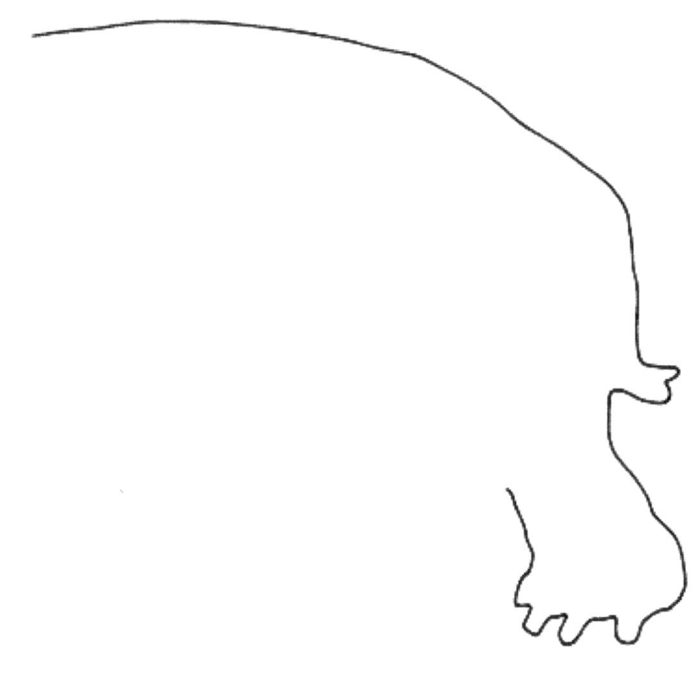

DOG

DOG
PRACTICE
AS SHOWN

DOG

PRACTICE
AS SHOWN

DOG

DRAW THE MISSING
LEVEL 1

DOG
DRAW THE MISSING
LEVEL 2

CONNECT THE DOTS 1 TO 26

DOG

DOG

PRACTICE AS SHOWN